ITALY

Little-Known FACTS

ABOUT

Well-Known PLACES

ITALY

DAVID HOFFMAN

METRO BOOKS
NEW YORK

Images: jupiterimages.com

Metro Books
122 Fifth Avenue
New York, NY 10011

ISBN: 978-1-4351-0429-7

Printed and bound in the United States of America

3 5 7 9 10 8 6 4 2

INTRODUCTION

Italy, Paris, New York...just hear their names and dozens of familiar images come to mind. But for everything that we may know about these (and other) favorite places, there is always a tidbit, a top secret, or a twist of fate that we have yet to discover.

Little-Known Facts about Well-Known Places goes beyond the obvious to reveal the stories behind the stories regarding the cities, countries, and tourist destinations that we all are familiar with—or at least think we're familiar with.

Covering every aspect—from food, film, and fashion to people, history, art, and architecture—these collections of offbeat facts and figures, statistics and specifics, are guaranteed to delight a first-time visitor and surprise even the most jaded local.

Packed with a wealth of revelations that could start (or stop) a conversation—not to mention win a ton of bar bets—*Little-Known Facts about Well-Known Places* is a must-have for know-it-alls, information addicts, curious readers, armchair travelers, and pop culture junkies of all ages.

Look for these other
titles in the series:

Little-Known
FACTS
ABOUT
Well-Known
PLACES

PARIS

NEW YORK

DISNEYLAND

IRELAND

It fluctuates, but the Tower of Pisa currently leans almost 13 feet to the south.

Modern-day pizza was invented when Don Raffaele Esposito, a Naples restaurant owner, layered a traditional flatbread with fresh tomatoes, mozzarella, and basil—ingredients he chose because they were red, white, and green, the colors of the Italian flag.

During the period from December 27 to December 31, store windows throughout Rome are filled with red boxer shorts, red underpants, and red lingerie. According to tradition, wearing red underwear on New Year's Eve and throwing it out the next day will insure good luck in the coming year.

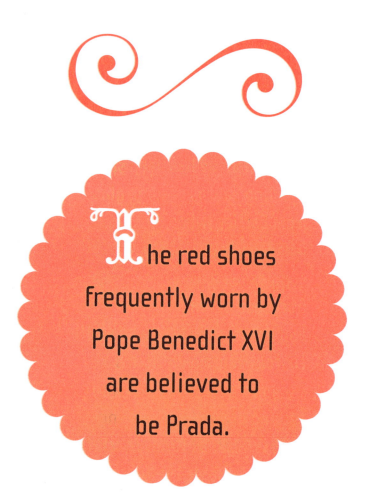

The red shoes frequently worn by Pope Benedict XVI are believed to be Prada.

Pope Benedict XVI definitely has an eye for fashion; he has been spotted sporting Santos reading glasses from Cartier (when he isn't wearing sunglasses from Gucci and Serengeti) and listening to his papal white, custom-engraved ("To His Holiness...") Apple iPod while rocking brown Geox walking shoes. All this brand association makes marketers very happy, given the pontiff's millions of devoted followers.

What's on Pope Benedict XVI's iPod? Works by Beethoven, Chopin, Tchaikovsky, and Stravinsky, plus a special twenty-minute feature on the life and music of Mozart that was produced just for him by the staff at Radio Vaticana. Benedict, a skilled pianist and big Mozart fan, is known to play a Mozart sonata before bedtime.

26

languages in which the radio station
at the Vatican broadcasts

.2

square mileage of Vatican City
(roughly 128 acres)

558

people who currently hold
Vatican City citizenship

0

income tax rate for citizens
of Vatican City

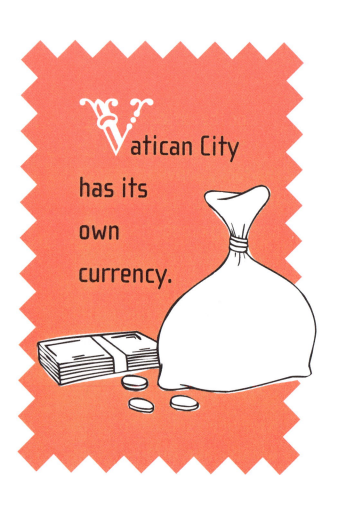

Vatican City has its own currency.

For the ultimate religious-themed goods, avoid the tacky souvenir stands that surround the Vatican and shop along the via dei Cestari, where the stores cater primarily to the clergy. At retailers like Gammarelli or Mancinelli, 12 bucks will get you the same iconic bright red socks that they have been selling to cardinals for six generations.

As soon as a new pope is elected, the requisite vestments must be immediately available to him, so that he can quickly put them on and step out onto the balcony overlooking St. Peter's Square. However, since no one knows in advance who the new pope is—and, hence, what size he is—ecclesiastical tailors must make and supply the Vatican with three complete sets of vestments—one small, one medium, and one large— to assure that they have one on hand that will fit.

$900

average price of a customized,
tailored cassock

$450

price of an off-the-rack cassock

33

buttons on a standard cassock

8

number of fabric panels sewn
together to make a zucchetto

The zucchetto, the small skullcap worn by clerics of the Roman Catholic Church, was first adopted for practical, not religious, reasons: the clerics had a ring of hair shaved, or tonsured, from the crown of the head as a symbol of their dedication to God, and the skullcap covered it to retain body heat in cold temperatures. In time, the color of the zucchetto—white, red, violet, black—would come to identify ecclesiastical rank.

The zucchetto gets its name from the Italian word *zucca*, meaning "pumpkin," because its eight panels stitched together and finished off with a "stem" at the top look exactly like one.

Rome's Antico Caffè Greco has been a favorite since 1760. Stendhal, Goethe, Byron, Shelley, Keats, and Casanova all sipped coffee there and, according to legend, any cardinal who enters and takes a seat will eventually become pope.

A series of 265 circular mosaic portraits that depict every pope since St. Peter are mounted in a continuous line on the frieze that runs above the columns and below the nave windows of the Basilica di San Paolo in Rome. Only the image of the current pope is illuminated, but visible just beyond that are a handful of vacant spots. The story goes that once they, too, have been filled, the world will come to an end.

Pope John Paul II had a rare blood type (AB), so he always traveled with containers of his own blood in case of emergency.

The pope's official bodyguards are Swiss citizens, between nineteen and thirty years old, at least 5 feet, 10 inches tall, and unmarried when they take the gig. The job description also requires that regardless of age they must be single for their first three years of duty, and if they are age twenty-one or younger, they must remain single until they have turned twenty-five.

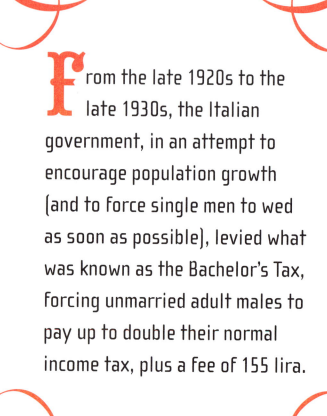

From the late 1920s to the late 1930s, the Italian government, in an attempt to encourage population growth (and to force single men to wed as soon as possible), levied what was known as the Bachelor's Tax, forcing unmarried adult males to pay up to double their normal income tax, plus a fee of 155 lira.

To offset the cost of the Parthian War, the Roman emperor Nero imposed a Urine Tax. The contents of some public latrines were collected by tanners and laundry workers because the ammonia in the urine made it useful for curing leather and bleaching togas. Nero's decision to tax the urine collectors was such a money-maker that when Vespasian succeeded him as emperor, he extended the practice to cover every public toilet. Hence, the Italian word for "urinal" is *vespasiano*.

There might be a shortage of public restrooms in Rome, but all those cafés (and there are a lot of them) are required by law to allow non-customers to use their facilities.

In almost any café in Italy, the price of coffee, a cocktail, or a glass of wine varies in relation to where you drink it: lowest if you order and stand at the bar, higher if you want to sit at a table, and highest if the table you choose is on the sidewalk

or terrace, rather than indoors.

Venice restaurants specialize in seafood from the Adriatic, but insiders know that the "fresh" fish listed on the menu of any restaurant that is open on Monday actually isn't. This is because the fish merchants at the city's famed Rialto Market take Sunday and Monday off; hence, unless the chef catches his own, any fish being served on Monday would have been purchased on Saturday.

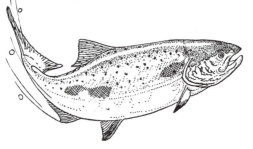

Trattoria Da Romano, a seafood restaurant in Burano, outside Venice, dates back to the early 1900s, and its original owners made it a practice of accepting paintings and sculpture as payment for meals. Over the years, the Italian artists who took them up on their offer included Gino Rossi, Umberto Moggioli, Pio Semeghini, Arturo Martini, and Luigi Scopinich, so the collection that hangs on the walls of the dining room is an impressive one.

A landlord who confiscated some of Modigliani's paintings in lieu of money for rent opted to use the canvases to patch old mattresses.

$10

maximum price paid, by today's economic standards, for a Modigliani painting during his lifetime (he died in 1920)

374

number of years after his death in 1519 before Botticelli was recognized as an important artist

60

percentage of existing art in the world that was created by Italians

637

number of *madonnelle* (images of the Virgin Mary, in frescoes, oil paintings, mosaics, and terracotta) currently found on the exterior walls and corners of buildings throughout Rome

When Christianity overtook Rome, mounted statues of emperors were considered pagan idols, and all of them—except for the equestrian imperial statue of Marcus Aurelius, now housed in the Capitoline Museum— were destroyed and melted down for coin. The Marcus Aurelius statue managed to escape ruin because a crusader wrongly identified it as a statue of Constantine, the emperor who made Christianity the new religion in the first place, and so left it intact.

The view of St. Peter's Square from via della Conciliazione is stunning, but the road has only been around since 1950. That's why locals urge first-time visitors to Rome to enter the Square the way it was first intended—from the side, through the oval colonnade—in order to experience the grandeur of the space, the spectacular facade, and the full impact of its beauty.

In a city that offers impressive vistas at every turn, the most unexpected (and most charming) view of Rome is from the piazza at the top of Aventine Hill. Don't let the locked gate or the walled compound of the Knights of Malta fool you. Just queue up in front of the ornate keyhole in the green door. It is purposely positioned so that what you see when you peek through is a picture-perfect view of St. Peter's Basilica, and Vatican City, several miles away.

ichard Meier's spectacular design for the Jubilee Church in Tor Tre Teste, 6 miles east of Rome, marks the first time that contemporary architecture has been applied to a religious building in Italy. It opened in 2003.

The Church of Sant'Ignazio in Rome, near the Pantheon, was built in the mid-seventeenth century without a cupola, because neighbors complained that a large dome would block their sun. So while the interior ceiling is flat, you would never discern that by looking up, thanks to an elaborate circular trompe l'œil fresco painted by Andrea Pozzo. It spans the nave where the dome would have been and creates the illusion that a cupola is actually there.

In a survey of artists, art historians, architects, architecture critics, designers, museum directors, and travel writers, it was unanimous: if you only have time to see one building in Rome, it should be the Pantheon. The gigantic round temple with the hemispheric dome is the best-preserved example of ancient architecture in the world, not to mention a masterpiece of technology and design.

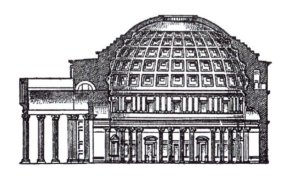

Although the Pantheon, built by the Romans, is made entirely of concrete, the type of rock used to form the concrete varied according to what part of the building was being constructed. Heavier stones, like travertine, were mixed in the concrete found in the lower portions and walls, and less dense rocks, like pumice, were used for the upper parts and dome, making them lighter, but still incredibly strong. That said, "light" is relative; the dome of the Pantheon weighs 5,000 tons.

The abbreviation for pound is "lb" because in ancient Rome, the value of a sack of coins was determined by weight, weight was measured in libras, and the libra, in records kept in Latin, was written as "lb."

It was common practice in the ancient marble quarries of Rome for unscrupulous stone dealers to cover any imperfections with wax. The ruse eventually became illegal, as the Roman Empire certified that all marble, in order to be genuine, had to be *sine cera*—or "without wax." Hence, to be sincere means to be genuine.

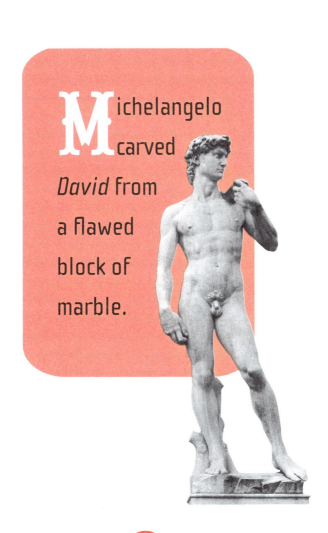

Michelangelo carved *David* from a flawed block of marble.

While the biblical David was Jewish—and therefore circumcised—the David portrayed in Michelangelo's statue is not. The most common theory for this difference is that the sculptor (as well as his model) was Roman Catholic, and he simply "drew what he knew."

The Pieta (found in St. Peter's Basilica) is the only work by Michelangelo that the artist ever signed. Having overheard someone attribute the piece to another sculptor, he supposedly snuck into the chapel at night and carved his name in the band running diagonally across Mary's chest to eliminate any question.

Michelangelo's wet nurse was the wife of a stonecutter; the artist claimed that he absorbed his passion for sculpting through her milk.

16 FEET, 10 INCHES

height of Michelangelo's *David*

2

sculptures whose attribution to Michelangelo
is still disputed

5,800

square footage of the Sistine Chapel ceiling
(yes, he painted every last inch)

4

years it took Michelangelo to paint the
Sistine Chapel, beginning in 1508

12

years it took to restore Michelangelo's painting
of the Sistine Chapel, beginning in 1980

Although the absolute best way to see the Sistine Chapel is from a prone position on the floor, the crowds make that pretty close to impossible. One tip: bring binoculars, which will let you check out this masterpiece as close up as humanly possible.

The Spanish Steps are actually French; the money to build them was bequeathed by a French diplomat's will and their primary purpose was to connect the piazza at the bottom with Trinita dei Monti, the church (which was under the patronage of the Bourbon Kings of France) at the top.

138

steps in the Spanish Steps

50

fountains fed by the waters of the
Aqua Virgo, including the Barcaccia
at the foot of the Spanish Steps
and the Trevi Fountain

€ 3,000

amount of money that is collected
nightly from the Trevi Fountain

It was only recently that the city of Rome began to collect the money tossed into the Trevi Fountain on a daily basis—and only after it was learned that a homeless man was regularly stealing the stash from the water using a magnetized pole. All Italian coins and euros end up in the coffers of the town council (most recently, they were used to subsidize a food bank); foreign currency is donated to the Red Cross.

The film *Three Coins in the Fountain* not only transformed a once-quiet piazza in Rome into a major tourist attraction, it also created a common misconception that three coins—not just one—should be tossed into the Trevi Fountain. So to set the record straight: throw one coin over your left shoulder using your right hand and you will return to the Eternal City. Throw two coins and you will soon be married. Throw three coins and your marriage will result in divorce.

The classic scene in *La Dolce Vita* where Anita Ekberg frolics in the Trevi Fountain was shot at night, in winter. According to director Federico Fellini, Ekberg had no trouble standing in the freezing water in a completely soaked dress, but Marcello Mastroianni needed to wear a wetsuit underneath his clothes. When even that failed to keep him warm, he resorted to shots of vodka—and, as a result, was completely drunk when he filmed the scene.

The term "paparazzi" comes from Fellini's *La Dolce Vita*; in the film, Marcello Mastroianni writes a gossip column and Walter Santesso plays his co-worker, a tabloid photographer whose name is Paparazzo.

In *The Agony and the Ecstasy*, the wet plaster that drips into the mouth of Michelangelo (played by Charlton Heston) is really chocolate pudding.

It was a family in Calabria—and their idea to cultivate broccoli—that financed the James Bond films. Albert R. "Cubby" Broccoli, who bought the initial rights to the Ian Fleming novels, and produced every 007 flick from *Dr. No* to *Golden Eye*, was an heir to the clan who had made a fortune when they crossed cauliflower and rabe and created a new vegetable they named for themselves.

Roman Holiday was the first American film to be made in its entirety in Rome. Paramount had frozen assets in Italy and the studio green-lighted the project specifically because filming there would allow those monies to be used.

Banks get their name from the word *bancu*, the Latin term for the long bench that moneylenders would set up in courtyards in ancient Rome, and from which they would do business.

$127 BILLION

money in the Italian economy generated
annually by organized crime

$43 BILLION

money organized crime takes in annually
just from interest on loans

7

percentage of Italy's gross domestic
product accounted for by organized crime

80

estimated percentage of the businesses
in the Sicilian cities of Catania and Palermo
that regularly pay the Mob *pizzo*
(protection money)

According to a type-written sheet of paper bearing the title "Rights and Duties" that was seized by the police when they apprehended crime boss Salvatore Lo Piccolo in 2007, members of the Italian mafia are bound by the following 10 commandments:

1. No one can present himself directly to another of our friends. There must be a third person to do it.
2. Never look at the wives of friends.
3. Never be seen with cops.
4. Don't go to pubs and clubs.
5. Always being available for Cosa Nostra is a duty—even if your wife's about to give birth.
6. Appointments must absolutely be respected.
7. Wives must be treated with respect.
8. When asked for any information, the answer must be the truth.
9. Money cannot be appropriated if it belongs to others or to other families.
10. People who can't be part of Cosa Nostra: anyone who has a close relative in the police, anyone with a two-timing relative in the family, anyone who behaves badly and doesn't hold to moral values.

The top place in Italy for having your pocket picked is on the No. 64 bus in Rome; its route runs between the Stazione Termini and St. Peter's Square (passing all of the "must see" historic sights). Thieves know that it is routinely packed with tourists. The easiest way not to look like a tourist? Local police suggest wearing a pair of oversized sunglasses.

Many of the streets in the historic center of Rome took their names from the specialty of the craftsmen who plied their trades there. Among them: via dei Giubbonari (jacket makers), via dei Chiavari (key makers), via dei Cappellari (hat makers), via dei Pettinari (comb makers), via dei Caellari (wigmakers), via dei Cartari (paper makers), and via dei Baullari (trunk makers).

Mass production in the nineteenth century devastated Italy's famed lace industry and most of what is sold today is either foreign or machine-made. Real Burano lace, made by hand, can be found, but it is intricate and rare; it takes a group of ten women up to three years to finish a tablecloth, and, on the low end, a 10-inch doily costs around $1,500.

Under Italian law, for an object to be labeled and sold as an antique, it need not be old, just made of old materials.

At the Museum of Roman Civilization (Museo della Civilta Romano), everything on display—from art and artifacts to sculptures, statues, and portions of monuments and buildings—is a reproduction in case of loss or destruction of the originals. Yet, so exact are these reproductions that they are revered as art in their own right.

Archaeologist and architect Italo Gismondi's famed plaster model of Rome, the chief attraction at the Museum of Roman Civilization, is built on a scale of 1:250 and represents the city in the fourth century, at the time of the emperor Constantine.

Dwarfs, who often doubled as jesters and servants, were an integral part of the Italian Renaissance court and lived in grand style in the homes of their employers. Probably the most unusual of the 500 rooms in the Ducale Palace in Mantua are the Apartments of the Dwarfs. Not only are they filled with custom-built furnishings designed to accommodate people of small stature, but at the center sits an exact replica of the Scala Santa (the Holy Stairs) in Rome, also perfectly scaled to the size of the residents.

19
roads that led to ancient Rome

53,000
miles of roads in ancient Rome

2.3 MILLION
square miles covered by the
Roman Empire at its territorial peak

250,000
seating capacity of Circus Maximus
during a chariot race

50,000
seating capacity of the Colosseum
during a gladiator fight

The Colosseum was built in an elliptical shape to prevent gladiators from retreating to corners and to allow the spectators an unobstructed view of all the action in the arena.

rena is Latin for "sand." Its use to denote the place where a sporting, theatrical, or musical event is held derives from the fact that in ancient Rome, when the hard-packed ground of the Colosseum could not soak up the blood spilled during a gladiator fight, the surface would be covered with sand to absorb it.

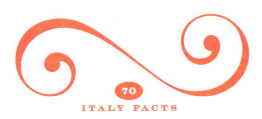

The huge travertine blocks of the Colosseum were once held in place by metal butterfly clamps; during the Middle Ages they were dug out and melted down for coin, leaving the Colosseum with its present pitted appearance. But that's okay: turns out, the large exterior blocks of travertine hold together simply by virtue of their own weight, an accidental (and early) example of dry wall construction.

The 200 feral cats that call the Colosseum home are protected by law, which stipulates that if a group of five or more felines are found living in a natural urban habitat (such as the city's ruins), they cannot be disturbed or removed. In total, Rome has 300,000 cats, more per capita than any other city in the world.

A thousand years before corrective lenses were invented, the Roman emperor Nero, in order to see the games in the Colosseum better, had a jeweler set a concave gem in a ring; he would watch the event by holding it up to one eye and focusing through it.

Fourteenth-century Venetian craftsmen, seeking a way to help those with poor vision, applied their glass-making expertise to the production of finely ground glass disks. They called them "lenses" because of their similarity in shape to lentils—*lens* being Latin for "lentil."

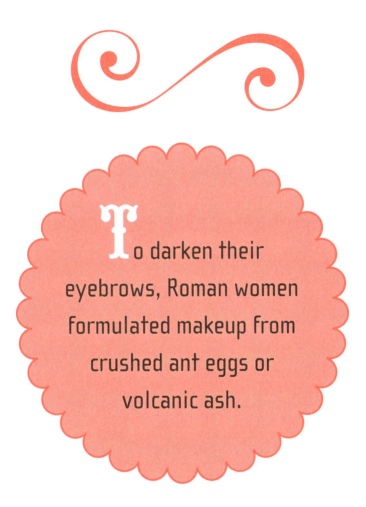

To darken their eyebrows, Roman women formulated makeup from crushed ant eggs or volcanic ash.

By the Numbers

19 HOURS

time it took Mt. Vesuvius to erupt and
destroy Pompeii in A.D. 79

700 DEGREES

temperature of lava released by
Mt. Vesuvius

70 MPH

speed of lava as it was released

40 FEET

depth of pumice and ash that
blanketed Pompeii

200

number of "wine bars" in Pompeii in A.D. 79
obliterated by Mt. Vesuvius

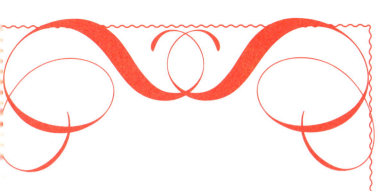

Lead has a natural sweetness, so ancient Romans used it to enhance both the color and bouquet of wine.

The juice that is pressed from most varieties of grapes is clear. Wine gets its color from the pigments in the skin of the grape—and whether or not (as well as for how long) those skins are left in contact with the juice during fermentation.

Chemists have identified over 250 compounds in wine, making it more complex than blood serum.

In Italy, it is considered unfeminine and improper for a woman to pour the wine.

80

bottles of wine the average Italian consumes per year

50 POUNDS

minimal pulling forced required to remove a cork from a bottle of wine using a waiter's corkscrew

600 TO 800

approximate number of grapes needed to produce a single bottle of wine

900,000

registered vineyards in Italy

1,000

grape varieties in Italy

In 1948, Giuseppe Cipriani, owner of Venice's famed Harry's Bar, wanted to take advantage of the abundance of white peaches available during the summer months, and concocted a cocktail that combined Prosecco, a local sparkling wine, with fresh peach puree. The unique shade of pink that resulted reminded him of the color of the toga worn by a saint in a favorite painting by Giovanni Bellini, so Cipriani named the drink Bellini in his honor.

When Countess Amalia Nani Mocenigo entered Harry's Bar in 1950, she announced that her doctor had put her on a diet forbidding cooked meat. To accommodate his customer's needs, Giuseppe Cipriani fixed up a plate consisting of thin slices of raw beef that he dressed with a light, cream-colored sauce. He called the dish *carpaccio*—in reference to sixteenth-century Renaissance artist Vittore Carpaccio—because the colors mirrored the Venetian painter's brilliant use of reds and whites in his work.

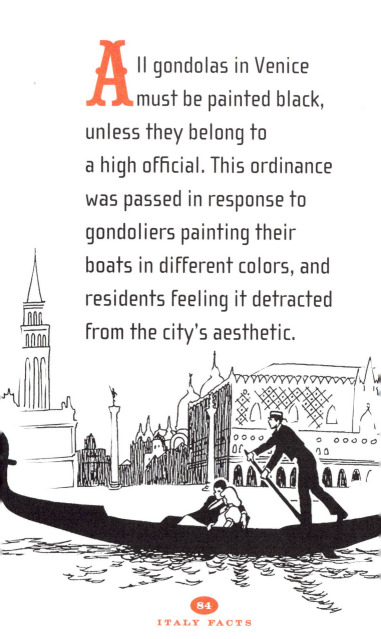

All gondolas in Venice must be painted black, unless they belong to a high official. This ordinance was passed in response to gondoliers painting their boats in different colors, and residents feeling it detracted from the city's aesthetic.

10,000

gondolas that plied the Venice canals in the fifteenth and sixteenth centuries

400

gondolas on the canals of Venice today

280

pieces of wood that go into handcrafting a new gondola

9

types of wood used to craft a gondola (beech, mahogany, cherry, elm, fir, larch, lime, oak, and walnut)

$35,000

approximate cost to build a gondola

Venice has had gondolas for more than a thousand years, but never a female gondolier.

(In 2007, the Locanda Art Deco Hotel *did* hire a woman to steer their private gondola, but she is not recognized by the gondolier's association, cannot officially call herself a gondolier, and, by law, is only allowed to paddle guests from that hotel.)

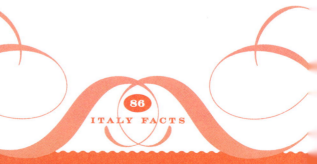

If you are going to lavish a small fortune (figure $120) on a gondola ride, the only worthwhile way to do it is at night, under the stars, once the day-trippers flocking to the city have left. Even better, request to be steered down the side waterways, away from the main canals.

2.3 MILES
length of Venice's Grand Canal

9 FEET
depth of the Grand Canal

50
since 1750, the average number of times Venice floods per year

20
plumbers listed in the Venice phonebook

etting lost in Venice is a given. Be prepared: Venetians do not give directions by streets or blocks, but in relation to bridges; for example "two bridges from here" or "after you've crossed the bridge, turn left."

90 MINUTES

time needed to walk from one end
of Venice to the other

400

footbridges in Venice

3,000

alleys in Venice

35 INCHES

width of Salizada de Ca'Zusto,
near the Byzantine church of
San Giacomo dell'Orio, the narrowest
of Venice's twisting alleys

There is definitely a photo op in the endless array of "inverted" chimney pots that dot the Venice skyline, but the real reason for their distinct shape is safety. Taking their design from the smoke stacks on early wood-burning steam trains, they were created to

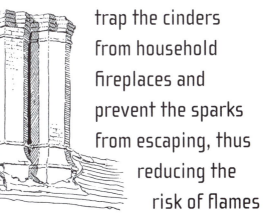

trap the cinders from household fireplaces and prevent the sparks from escaping, thus reducing the risk of flames spreading to adjoining buildings.

184,000

population of Venice in 1950

60,000

population of Venice in 2008

1,000

average number of residents who move out of Venice each year

450

souvenir shops in Venice

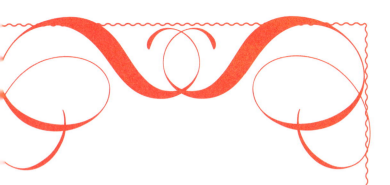

The first printing of the Koran was done in Venice around 1547 by Alessandro Paganino. However, Paganino did not know Arabic, so his text was riddled with mistakes.

Tintoretto's *Paradise*, which hangs over the Grand Council chamber in the Palazzo Ducale in Venice, measures 74' x 30', and is believed to be the largest painting ever done on canvas.

Leonardo DiCaprio was named after artist Leonardo da Vinci; apparently, his pregnant mother was standing in front of a Leonardo painting at the Uffizi museum in Florence when she first felt DiCaprio kick.

Leonardo da Vinci should have been known as Leonardo da Anchiano since he was born in Anchiano, a small village in the town of Vinci.

Leonardo da Vinci was a perfectionist (and a procrastinator), so while his legacy includes hundreds of drawings and sketches, he only left behind thirty paintings— many unfinished.

Leonardo da Vinci was an accomplished lyre player and gained attention as a musician long before he was ever recognized as an artist or inventor.

In addition to being a master violinist and a renowned composer (he produced over 600 works in his lifetime), Antonio Vivaldi was also, at the age of twenty-three, an ordained priest—perhaps because, coming from a poor family, studying for the priesthood was one way he could attend school for free.

ivaldi's

The Four Seasons is the top-selling classical music recording of all time.

Luciano Pavarotti was working as an elementary school teacher in his hometown of Modena when the local amateur chorus he sang with took first place at a music competition in Wales, convincing him he might have a future in opera.

9

number of high C's Pavarotti could hit effortlessly in a single aria

17

curtain calls Pavarotti received after a 1972 performance of "La Fille du Regiment"

11 MINUTES

length of the standing ovation Pavarotti received after his final performance in 2004

100 MILLION

combined number of albums and collections that Pavarotti has sold, making him classical music's most successful recording artist

$15 MILLION

amount Pavarotti paid the Italian government in fines after charges of tax evasion

According to the *Wall Street Journal Europe*, traders commonly opt to substitute slang for numbers to avoid any costly misunderstandings. On the floor of the London stock exchange, "Pavarotti" is dealer shorthand for "10." Figure it this way: the Italian opera singer was a tenor, tenor is a homonym for "tenner," and in England "tenner" is a colloquial term for a £10 note.

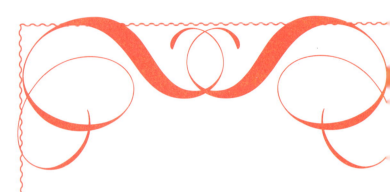

Ballet is rooted in the late fifteenth century Italian Renaissance where it surfaced as a dance interpretation of fencing.

The volume of a harpsichord cannot be regulated, so in an attempt to improve on it, Bartolomeo Cristofori, who was employed by Prince Ferdinand de Medici as the Keeper of the Instruments, invented a version where amplitude could be changed according to the amount of pressure on the keys. He called the new instrument the piano, short for *pianoforte*, which translates to "soft-loud."

Castelfidardo, a small town in Le Marche, is "The Accordion Capital of the World" and home to more than thirty manufacturers who produce a total of 15,000 handmade instruments a year.

1,101

estimated number of instruments made by
Antonio Stradivari in his lifetime

650

Stradivarius instruments known
to have survived

200 HOURS

average time it took Stradivari
to make a violin

$3,544,000

amount paid, at a May 16, 2006 auction,
for a Stradivarius called The Hammer

11

Stradivarius violins owned by violin virtuoso
Nicolo Paganini at the time of his death in 1840

Two of the more popular explanations for the unparalleled acoustics of a Stradivarius violin are that Stradivari worked Pozzolana earth, a volcanic ash, into the varnish and that the spruce wood he used had been soaked in salt water.

In the fifteenth century—more than 400 years before Rontgen accidentally discovered the X-ray—violin string was used to diagnose skull fractures. The amazingly accurate technique was the creation of Guido Lanfranc, a Milan surgeon; he would have a patient bite down on the end of a violin string, which he would then stretch tight and strum. If the musical note that resulted was vivid and clear, the skull was fine; however, if the sound was dull and garbled, then the patient had suffered a fracture.

Renaissance man Girolamo Fracastoro, a physician and poet, authored an epic piece about a shepherd—named Syphilis—who was infected with (as it was known in Italy) *morbus gallicus* ("the disease of the French"). As a result of the poem's notoriety, the illness became universally known as "Syphilis' disease," and eventually, simply "syphilis."

A hundred years before they became the rage in seventeenth-century England, a condom was invented in Padua by Gabriel Fallopius (the same doctor who had identified, explained, and then named the two tubes that carry ova from the ovaries to the uterus). His medicated linen sheaths (which he called "overcoats") came available in one size—8 inches— and tied securely at the base of the penis with a pink ribbon. (Pink, he deduced, would give them added appeal to the women who would be seeing them.)

In order to avoid the inevitable consequences that could result from all the sex he was having, legendary lothario Giacomo Girolamo Casanova used lemons as his method of contraception. He would cut the fruit in half, then scoop out the pulp; the rind doubled as a cervical cap and the acidic juice was a powerful spermicide. The idea actually has validity—modern day clinical tests have proven that the natural acids in lemon juice do kill sperm, and can be an effective weapon against HIV.

A young priest named Valentine disagreed with the Roman emperor's edict abolishing marriage and continued to perform wedding ceremonies in secret. When Claudius II discovered that he was doing this, he ordered Valentine's execution. Imprisoned and awaiting his fate, Valentine fell for the blind daughter of the jailer and in classic love story fashion, his undying devotion restored her sight. But it was his passion-filled farewell message to her—which he signed "From Your Valentine"—that made romantic history.

Becoming so overwhelmed by Italy's abundance of beauty, art, culture, and history that you develop a rapid heart rate, shortness of breath, and lightheadedness is the sign of a medical condition known as Stendhal Syndrome. The name comes from Stendhal, the French writer, who collapsed outside the Basilica di Santa Croce in Florence the first time he saw it, he was that overcome by its brilliance.

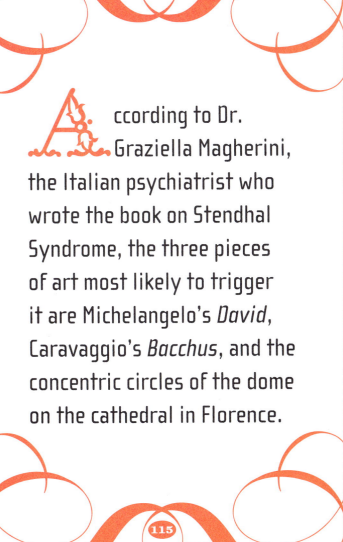

According to Dr. Graziella Magherini, the Italian psychiatrist who wrote the book on Stendhal Syndrome, the three pieces of art most likely to trigger it are Michelangelo's *David*, Caravaggio's *Bacchus*, and the concentric circles of the dome on the cathedral in Florence.

Caravaggio's *Bacchus* hangs in the Uffizi Gallery in Florence and features the god of wine reclining seductively, with grapes and vine leaves in his hair. While the portrait screams classic Italian Baroque, it does not take itself as seriously as other paintings of the age: on the stone table in front of Bacchus is a carafe of red wine. Examine it closely and you'll see a tiny self-portrait of the artist working at his easel in the reflection on the glass.

he model and plans presented by Filippo Brunelleschi that won him the commission to design the dome and cupola for the cathedral in Florence in 1419 had enough detail to serve as a guide for the craftsmen, but he cleverly omitted a few specifics to ensure he could maintain control over the construction.

There is an unexploded bomb beside the confessionals in the Cattedrale di San Lorenzo Campanile in Genoa. The British dropped it on the city during World War I, but it never went off—and no one has ever removed it.

In most cities in Italy, the building that defines the skyline is a cathedral. La Mole Antonellian—the structure so identified with Turin that it appears on the back of the 2-cent Italian euro, was the symbol of the 2006 Winter Olympic Games, and is now the spectacular home to the National Museum of Cinema— also has religious roots; only it was originally intended to be a synagogue.

Chocolate was very expensive and available only to the wealthy as a beverage until a Frenchman named Doret, living in Turin, invented a machine that could grind cacao seeds into a paste, and solid chocolate was born. This was the mid-seventeenth century and eating chocolate, as opposed to drinking it, was big. So big, that Doret's recipes were classified as state secrets.

Diablotins—small drops rolled from cocoa paste—were one of the first solid chocolates produced in Turin. Though tasty, they proved to be quite messy to eat and unable to hold up for export. Cleverly, a candy maker rolled them in sugary pellets to stop them from melting in the hand before they could melt in the mouth. Over time, the chocolates would become better known by the name of their candy coating: *nonpareils*.

Turin may produce more chocolate annually than France and Germany combined, but it is not the only chocolate center in Italy. A relatively undiscovered area of Tuscany, about 40 miles west of Florence, has recently been dubbed the Chocolate Valley because of the high concentration of high-end chocolatiers—including Amedei, Paul de Bondt, Roberto Catinari, and Luca Mannori—based there.

Since 2005, the Committee of Experts of the London Academy of Chocolate has taste-tested over 300 brands of chocolate, and for three years in a row, the Toscano Black 63 percent bar made by Amedei, a chocolatier located outside Pisa and owned by a brother and sister team, has been selected as the best chocolate in the world.

Chocolate hazelnut paste, generally known as *gianduia* and branded commercially as Nutella, was developed out of frustration when the Napoleonic Wars made it impossible to get cacao beans in Italy. Michele Prochet ground hazelnuts, which were plentiful in the Piedmont area where he lived, with cacao beans in equal parts to make his stash last twice as long.

For 200 years, *gianduia*—chocolate blended with hazelnut—has been one of Italy's signature flavors. The name comes from Gianduja, a popular marionette character with a predilection for wine, gastronomy, and beautiful women. Gianduja is the mascot of Turin, where the flavor combo was first invented, and his mask is a fixture at Carnevale in nearby Ivrea.

Those that gather annually for Carnevale in Ivrea mark the celebration leading up to Lent with a three-day battle during which they throw oranges at one another. About 10,000 people take part, going through close to 600,000 pounds of oranges; the pulp gets so deep that snow-removal equipment is needed to clear it.

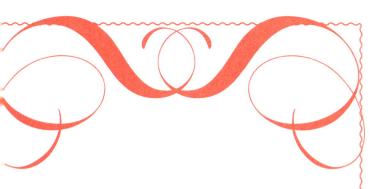

In the sixteenth century, after much debate, the Vatican categorized liquid chocolate as a nutritional substitute and deemed it okay to drink during Lent and other fasting periods.

In 2007, the Vatican launched Mistral Air, a low-cost charter airline to fly pilgrims from Rome to religious sites around the world. The venture hit its first snag on the return portion of its inaugural trip to Lourdes, when passengers carrying holy water were denied boarding. Apparently, the Virgin Mary-shaped water bottles held more than was permitted by security restrictions.

For a bottled water in Italy to be classified as *acqua minerale* ("mineral water"), it must pass a complicated series of chemical analyses, all regulated by law. Labels list mineral contents and identify the specific medicinal properties of the springs from which the water is collected. Hence, consumers purchase different brands for different purposes, such as Crodo for dyspepsia, or Neri for preventing hangovers.

600

brands of mineral water bottled
in Italy

40 DAYS

recommended period of time lemon
peel should soak in pure alcohol in a
dark place, in order to make limoncello

20 PERCENT

amount of all the liquor sold in
Italy that is grappa

50

varieties of herbs and spices used
to infuse vermouth

Vermouth was first created in 1786 by an employee of a liquor store in Turin who, attempting to salvage a barrel of moscato wine that was starting to oxidize, added herbs and spices according to the dictates of the monks who lived nearby.

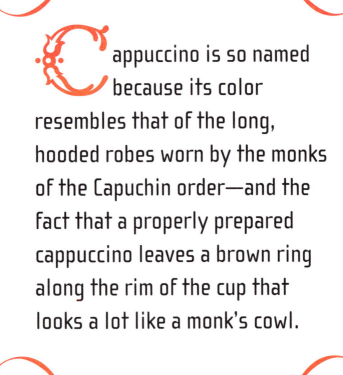

Cappuccino is so named because its color resembles that of the long, hooded robes worn by the monks of the Capuchin order—and the fact that a properly prepared cappuccino leaves a brown ring along the rim of the cup that looks a lot like a monk's cowl.

Real cappuccino is made with whole milk, steamed lightly, and rarely consumed after midday. Terms like non-fat and soy will draw blank stares in Italy. Other tips to remember: order "coffee" and you will get an espresso; order "latte" and you will get a glass of milk. Definitely steer clear of saying "venti"—unless you really want twenty coffees.

The name espresso derives from both *esprimere*, which is Italian for "pressed out," and from the fact that the coffee was initially sold to commuters as they boarded the express train in Milan.

Although women were often expected to keep their heads covered, it was not until the seventeenth century that women's headgear emerged as a fashion statement. The haberdashers that designed, made, and sold hats (along with ribbons and buttons and other fineries) were based in Milan; hence, these manufacturers were known as Milaners, from which *milliner*, the common term for hat maker, is derived.

The modern day uniform for the Italian Air Force was designed by Giorgio Armani.

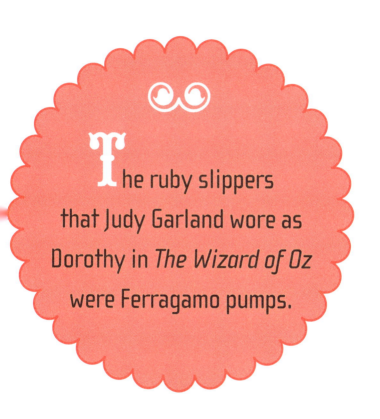

The ruby slippers that Judy Garland wore as Dorothy in *The Wizard of Oz* were Ferragamo pumps.

By the Numbers

3

museums in Italy devoted solely to footwear

10,000

pairs of shoes in the collection of the
Ferragamo Shoe Museum in Florence
(150 to 180 are displayed at one time)

250

pairs of Ferragamo flats, in different colors
and fabrics but all in the same style, found in
Leona Helmsley's closet at the time of her death

2,700

small shoe factories in the Le Marche region of
Italy, all within a 125-square-mile area

133

rubber pebbles on the sole of a
Tod's Gommino moccasin

In 1978, Dorino Della Valle was making shoes for U.S. department stores (under the stores' labels) from his studio in Casette d'Ete when his son Diego suggested they take a basic, utilitarian piece of footwear, turn it into a luxury item, and brand it as their own. To name the new business, Diego opened a Boston phone book and randomly picked a listing that sounded right: J.P. Tod. They launched the product line with a moccasin-turned-leather driving shoe, which in no time drove an empire.

Italy boasts more cars, per person, than any other nation in the world, with 32 million vehicles for 57 million people.

0

cars in Venice

500,000

people who get around Rome on moped

30

mopeds stolen in Rome each day

36

Ferrari 250 GTO models produced
in the early 1960s

$18,000

sticker price of a Ferrari 250 GTO in 1962

$5.5 MILLION

price paid at auction for a Ferrari 250 GTO
in 1991

When Ferruccio Lamborghini, a tractor manufacturer, complained about the faulty clutch in his Ferrari 250 GTO, Enzo Ferrari refused to do anything about it. So Lamborghini took it upon himself to dismantle the GTO clutch and discovered that it was made by the same firm that supplied the heavy-duty clutches for his tractors. A simple swap of the two clutches followed, and the problem was solved. Sort of. Determined to teach Ferrari a lesson, Lamborghini started his own car company.

Ferruccio Lamborghini was a much better car designer than he was a driver. The first time he got behind the wheel of one of his namesake vehicles, he ended up crashing it through the front of a café. When the owner rushed over and asked if he was okay, Lamborghini is said to have looked up and remarked, "I just stopped in to order some red wine...."

The logo for Lamborghini is a charging bull, maybe because Ferruccio Lamborghini was a Taurus, but definitely because he had a passion for bulls and bull-fighting. So much so that practically every model of Lamborghini is named for a breed of bull, if not a particular bull.

The trident at the center of the Maserati logo is an homage to the trident that figures prominently in the classic Fountain of Neptune near Piazza Maggiore in Bologna—the city where the company's cars were first manufactured.

Fiat is Italy's largest single employer; the name is an acronym for Fabbrica Italiana Automobili Torino (Italian Automobile Factory of Turin), but it also means "let there be" in Latin.

iat's Punto was named "European Car of the Year," but when the vehicle was launched in South America, sales failed to meet analysts' expectations—probably due to the fact that "punto" is local slang for the male organ.

St. Francesca Romana is the patron saint of motorists and every year on March 9, her feast day, Roman drivers flock to the traffic circle around the Colosseum to seek her protection. With traditional ceremony, a cardinal stands in a safe place and blesses, with a sprinkle of holy water, the lines of cars, trucks, buses, and city vehicles as they pass. After he makes the sign of the cross, drivers respond with a blast of their horns or sirens and move on, fully protected.

While the pope uses a variety of Popemobiles, all of them donated by Mercedes-Benz, the model seen in recent papal travels (including Pope Benedict XVI's 2008 trip to the United States) is a customized two-door M-Class ML 430, with mother of pearl finish and white interior appointments.

The personalized license plate on the Popemobile reads "SCV 1." The letters stand for Stato Città del Vaticano, which is the Vatican's name in Italian; the number "1" refers to the Holy Father's position in the church hierarchy.

272

horsepower of the Popemobile

8 SECONDS

time it takes the Popemobile to go from zero to 60 mph

6 FEET

height of the glass enclosure built to showcase the pontiff

3

passengers, other than the driver and the pope, that the Popemobile can carry

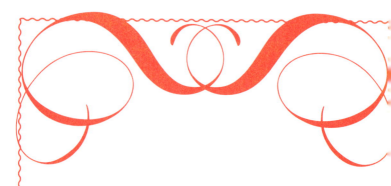

In the thirteenth century, the Pope established quality standards for pasta—including that dried pasta could only be made with durum wheat semolina—that still apply today.

Although Marco Polo usually gets the credit for introducing pasta to Italy, it was the Arabs 500 years earlier who, during their conquest of Sicily, carried pasta with them as a dry staple. If Marco did bring back something with him from his travels to China, it was most likely techniques for making fresh, stuffed pasta, which explains why making tortellini is virtually identical to making wonton.

The fork was invented in Tuscany as a utensil with which to eat pasta, although it was unilaterally dismissed by the clergy, who frowned upon using anything not created by God to touch God's bounty.

Italian etiquette in the 1500s specified that people were supposed to eat with their hands, and that there were right and wrong ways to do it. Picking up food with just the thumb and the first two fingers—and being particularly careful not to dirty the ring finger and the pinky—was a sure sign of proper breeding, but dining using all five fingers was considered uncouth.

With the growing acceptance and more common usage of the fork by the early 1600s (gold and silver versions, in particular, had become a status symbol among the wealthy), Galileo designed a comb that could double as an eating utensil, demonstrating why he was better known for astronomy than gastronomy.

Italians consider it proper etiquette to eat pasta with a fork, but not a fork and a spoon. What experts suggest instead is that pasta be served in wide, shallow bowls, as the sides of the bowl provide a surface against which the noodles can be turned on the fork.

61 POUNDS

amount of pasta that the average person
in Italy eats per year

92 POUNDS

amount of pasta that the average
Sicilian eats per year

600

number of shapes of pasta

6.5 BILLION

gallons of water (enough to fill 250,000
Olympic-size swimming pools) needed
to boil all the pasta consumed in
Italy each year

Most commercial pastas today are extruded through Teflon molds and dried quickly, while the best brands are made using bronze dies. These higher quality pastas have a visibly mottled surface and are rough to the touch. When cooked, they hold the sauce better.

Tomatoes are a member of the nightshade family—most of which are poisonous—so for almost 200 years after they were brought from Mexico to Europe, Italians were afraid to eat them. Instead, they kept them as houseplants.

While on honeymoon in Rome in 1927, Mary Pickford and Douglas Fairbanks dined every night at Alfredo's restaurant on chef/owner Alfredo di'Lelio's *fettucine al buro*, a dish he made with pasta, butter, and cream. When they brought the recipe back with them to Hollywood, they shared it freely, but to honor the man who had created it, they took to calling it *fettucine Alfredo*.

The origin of *spaghetti alla carbonara* can be traced to the end of World War II, when U.S. soldiers shared their bacon and egg rations with the Italians they had just liberated—who then got the idea to mix it with pasta.

Olive oil is better for cooking than other types of oil since it burns at a higher temperature.

1 PERCENT

maximum acidity allowed for olive oil
to be classified as "extra virgin"

60

number of raw oysters Casanova
reportedly ate daily

12 INCHES

maximum diameter allowable for a pizza
according to guidelines set forth by
the Naples Pizza Association

9 PERCENT

fat content of buffalo's milk (water buffalo,
not the American bison) used to make
traditional mozzarella (for the record:
cow's milk has a fat content of 3.5 percent)

When a young man working for a cheesemaker in Lombardy in the thirteenth century skipped out early one afternoon to spend time with his girlfriend, he attempted to cover his tracks the next morning by throwing the previous day's batch of unfinished *stracchino* into the containers holding the new milk supply. The pungent smell and blueish-green color of the resulting curd gave him away. What saved him is that everyone who tried it loved the taste. He named the new cheese Gorgonzola, in honor of the tiny town where he lived.

Fava beans were used as cattle feed until a drought in Sicily wiped out all the wheat fields and people started eating them. Grateful for any food at all, they also began to think of a fava bean as a symbol of good luck. Hence, Italians say that a pantry that contains a fava bean will never be bare, and that people who carry a fava bean in their pocket or purse will always have money.

Thousands of years ago, Italians believed that fowl could predict the future, based on the fact that the hen's cluck foretold of an egg and the rooster's crow signaled the dawn. Since the collarbone was thought to give the bird its powers, it was saved as a symbol of luck. Occasionally, fights would break out over these "wish bones" and they would be broken in the process. From this, we get both the practice of breaking the wishbone and the expression "lucky break."

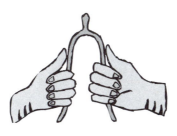

In Italy, the number seventeen is unlucky. When written using the Roman numerals XVII, the letters are an anagram of VIXI (meaning "I have lived"), which is commonly found on ancient tombstones. If seventeen is written using the Arabic numerals 17, it is still considered bad luck, since it resembles a man hanging from the gallows.

The "Hook 'Em Horns" rallying call for the University of Texas Longhorns football team takes on new meaning in Italy, where raising a fist with the index and little fingers extended is a hardcore insult; a graphic way of telling a man that his wife or girlfriend is sleeping around. The hand signal might also be misinterpreted as a satanic symbol—something five Americans learned in 1985 when they were arrested for making the sign in front of the Vatican while celebrating news of a Longhorns victory.

There is a long standing cultural tradition whereby Italian men, when hearing bad news or seeing something that portends bad news (such as a hearse) put their hands in front of their crotches and say *"Io mi tocco"*—or, "I touch myself"—which is similar (at least in theory) to crossing their fingers.

Many Italians believe that nuns bring bad luck. As soon as they see one, they will either immediately touch iron—similar to "knocking on wood" —or they will mutter "Your nun!" at the next person they see, thereby passing the bad luck on to them.

In 1999, a group of nuns from the convent of San Casa di Nazareth, in Passirano, Lombardy, recorded a rap album under the name Sister Act; their song *Your Nun, Touch Iron* cleverly protested the traditional belief that seeing a nun brings bad luck.

L'Eau Vive, a well-reviewed French restaurant on via Monterone in Rome, has received one Michelin star (try the pâté…), but its true distinction lies in the fact that all of the waitresses are nuns.

The Great Council of Venice declared prostitution to be "absolutely indispensable to the world" in 1358, and brothels, backed by the government, were established throughout the area. By the end of the century, there were 2,500 nuns in Venice…and

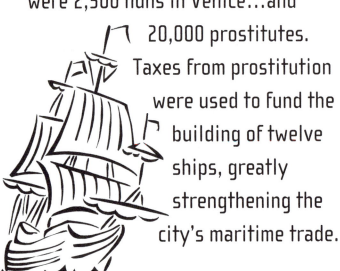

20,000 prostitutes. Taxes from prostitution were used to fund the building of twelve ships, greatly strengthening the city's maritime trade.

It is illegal to be a prostitute in Siena if your name is Mary.

When the Venetian Republic issued an edict in the mid-1400s forbidding dueling with swords to the death, the enlightened Italian state ruled that matters of differences should be settled instead with a game of chess.

Up until 1527, Jews in Venice lived in the isolated Cannaregio district on the site of an abandoned foundry where artillery had been cast. Because the Italian word meaning "to cast" is *gettare*, locals began to refer to the area as "ghetto," and it was from this that the term obtained its modern meaning.

Despite their name, venetian blinds didn't originate in Venice. They were the brainchild of Edward Beran, an eighteenth-century British inventor. He called them "venetian" because at the time he created them, Italian furnishings were considered very sophisticated.

Glow-in-the-dark toys date back to the 1600s and were the innovation of Vincenzo Cascariolo, a cobbler from Bologna who dabbled in alchemy—and who accidentally discovered chemiluminescence when he failed to figure out how to turn lead into gold.

A unit of electricity is called a volt in honor of Alessandro Volta, the Italian physicist who developed the first electric battery.

Guglielmo Marconi, the inventor best known for his development of the wireless radio, was (through his Irish mother) an heir to the Jameson whiskey fortune.

Balsamic vinegar was originally produced by prosperous families of Modena and the Emilia-Romagna region for their own pleasure, and was revered for its healing properties and savored like an aperitif. Often given as a gift, it was never intended to be bottled for commercial use.

Balsamic vinegar may be aged for 100 years (and has been around for thousands), but it is only in the last twenty-five years that it has been known outside the area where it is produced. Interestingly, this culinary craze was started by American businessman Chuck Williams, who brought some home from Modena in 1976 to sell at his flagship Williams-Sonoma store in San Francisco.

Most vinegar labeled balsamic actually isn't. Rather, it is a balsamic vinegar made somewhere other than Modena or the Emilia-Romagna region, a younger Modena vinegar (meaning it has not been aged the minimum requisite number of years to be balsamic), or a commercially produced vinegar in the style of balsamic vinegars.

12 YEARS

minimum amount of time vinegar must be
aged to qualify as balsamic

5

number of grape varieties that may be
used to make balsamic vinegar

$100 TO $400

average price of a small bottle of the
highest quality balsamic vinegar

8,000

maximum number of bottles of DOC
designated balsamics (3.36 ounces each)
that the Consortium of the Producers of
Traditional Balsamic Vinegar of Modena
stipulates can be produced annually

The DOC designation given to Italian wine, cheese, olive oil, and balsamic vinegar translates to mean "denomination of controlled origin," a classification system that sets production standards for a number of foods. This is not a guarantee of excellence, just a guarantee that certain standards of production were met. That said, it is pretty much a given that following these guidelines will result in excellence.

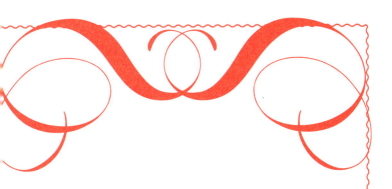

Throughout Italy,
picking the teeth
with a toothpick after dinner
is a sign that the meal
was appreciated.

The experienced eater of *focaccia* can tell what city it comes from by how it is made. In Florence, it is baked plain, then once removed from the oven, topped with things that do not require heat, such as fresh tomatoes. In the Liguria region, it is sprinkled with salt and coated with extra virgin olive oil before baking. In the city of Carrara in Tuscany, it has chopped walnuts in the dough. In Viareggio in Tuscany, it is flavored with malt. And in the Lombardy region, it is sweetened with sugar.

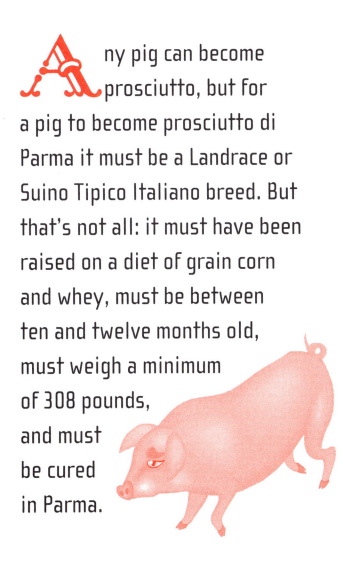

Any pig can become prosciutto, but for a pig to become prosciutto di Parma it must be a Landrace or Suino Tipico Italiano breed. But that's not all: it must have been raised on a diet of grain corn and whey, must be between ten and twelve months old, must weigh a minimum of 308 pounds, and must be cured in Parma.

While prosciutto di Parma ham is (by law) cured for four months, then hung to dry for at least 300 days, the U.S. Department of Agriculture demands that any ham imported to the United States must hang for 400 days. Reportedly, the additional 100 days makes for a richer, more flavorful product. So, when all is cured and dried, it is possible that the prosciutto in the United States is even better than that in Italy.

While his work—which includes the spectacular grotto that adjoins the Boboli Gardens and the Pitti Palace in Florence, as well as the Belvedere (the fort that protected the palace and the city)—is impressive, architect and impresario Bernardo Buontalenti's biggest cultural impact was introducing gelato to Italy.

The canning process for herring was developed in Sardinia, which is why canned herring are more commonly called sardines.

A muskmelon that was brought from Armenia to Italy in the fifteenth century was planted and cultivated in the gardens of a papal estate near Rome. The estate was Cantaluppi, so the fruit crop that resulted became known as cantaloupe.

Harry Pickering was a rich kid from Boston who, while living in Venice, eventually found himself broke and cut off from his family. Giuseppe Cipriani, who ran the bar where Pickering spent most of his nights (and his money) decided to help out and generously loaned him 10,000 lire so he could pay his hotel bill and get home. Two years later, Pickering returned to Venice, walked into the bar, handed 10,000 lire to Cipriani, thanked him—and then gave him 40,000 more. "It is enough to open a bar," he explained, knowing this was something Giuseppe always wanted to do. "You will call it Harry's Bar." And Cipriani did.

*C*iao! derives from *schiavo*—the Italian word for slave—meaning "I am here to serve." The greeting, however, was not meant to be taken literally; rather it was intended as a show of good will, as in, "Know that I'm here for you."

Ernest Hemingway's novel *A Farewell to Arms*, which tells the story of an American serving as an ambulance driver in the Italian army during World War I, is credited with bringing the word *ciao* into the English language.

Shakespeare used Italian settings in at least 13 of his plays—*All's Well that Ends Well*, *Antony and Cleopatra*, *Coriolanus*, *Cymbeline*, *Julius Caesar*, *The Merchant of Venice*, *Much Ado About Nothing*, *Othello*, *Romeo and Juliet*, *The Taming of the Shrew*, *Titus Andronicus*, *The Two Gentlemen of Verona*, and *The Winter's Tale*— yet, in his lifetime, he never once visited "The Boot."

ABOUT THE AUTHOR

David Hoffman is a television writer, a frequent on-camera correspondent, and the author of over a dozen books about popular culture, for which, in recent years, he has been paid to play with toys, challenge untapped cooking skills (with the help of some big-name chefs), and eat and shop his way across the country. He lives in Los Angeles, where he likes to pretend this is hard work.

DISCLAIMER

All facts, figures, statistics, stories, quotes, and anecdotes found on these pages were checked (and double-checked) and believed to be true (or have some semblance of truth) at the time the book went to press. But things change; stuff happens. So cut me some slack if they're not.

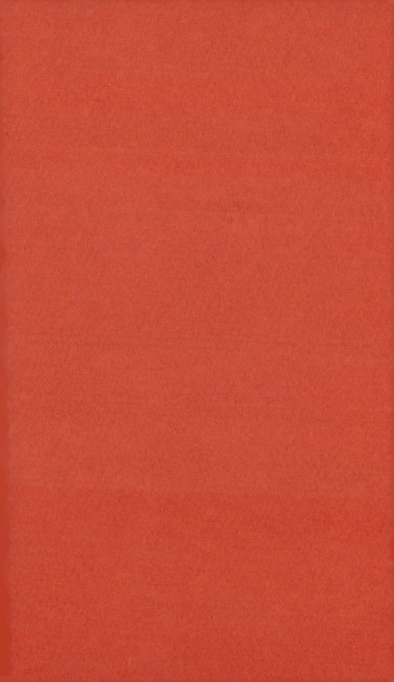